ALL TIME HEROES

FROM ALL TIMES

~ Volume 2 ~

ALL TIME HEROES

FROM ALL TIMES

~ Volume 2 ~

THE LIFE OF MARTIN
BISHOP OF TOURS

by St Sulpitius Severus

ST SHENOUDA'S MONASTERY
SYDNEY, AUSTRALIA
2013

All Time Heroes From All Times - Volume 2
THE LIFE OF ST MARTIN BISHOP OF TOURS

COPYRIGHT © 2013
St. Shenouda Monastery

ST SHENOUDA MONASTERY
8419 Putty Rd,
Putty, NSW, 2330
Sydney, Australia

www.stshenoudamonastery.org.au

ISBN 13: 978-0-9873400-4-7

Cover Design:
Hani Ghaly,
Begoury Graphics
begourygraphics@gmail.com

Contents

Life and Writings of Sulpitius Severus   9
Preface to Desiderius   15
Reasons for Writing the Life of St. Martin   17
Military Service of St. Martin   21
Christ Appears to St. Martin   25
Martin Retires from Military Service   29
Martin Converts a Robber to the Faith.   33
The Devil Throws Himself in the Way of Martin

                                               37
Martin Restores a Catechumen to Life.   41
Martin Restores one that had been Strangled.   45
High Esteem in which Martin was held.   47
Martin as Bishop of Tours.   51
Martin Demolishes an Altar Consecrated to a
Robber.   55
Martin Causes the Bearers of a Dead Body to Stop.

                                               57
Martin Escapes from a Falling Pine-tree.   59
Martin Destroys Heathen Temples and Altars.

                                               63
Martin Offers his Neck to an Assassin.   67
Cures Effected by St. Martin.   69
Martin Casts out Several Devils.   73
Martin Performs Various Miracles.   77
A Letter of Martin Effects a Cure, with Other
Miracles.   79
How Martin Acted towards the Emperor Maximus.

                                               81
Martin has to do Both with Angels and Devils.

                                               85

Martin Preaches Repentance even to the Devil.

87

A Case of Diabolic Deception   *91*

Martin is Tempted by the Wiles of the Devil.   *95*

Intercourse of Sulpitius with Martin.   *99*

Words Cannot Describe the Excellences of Martin.

103

Wonderful Piety of Martin.   *105*

How St. Martin passed from this Life to Life Eternal.   *107*

LIFE AND WRITINGS OF SULPITIUS SEVERUS

Sulpitius (or Sulpicius) Severus was born in Aquitania about 363 AD, and died, as is generally supposed, in 420 AD. He was thus a contemporary of the two great Fathers of the Church, St. Jerome and St. Augustine. The former refers to him in his Commentary on the 36th chapter of Ezekiel as "our friend Severus." St. Augustine, again, having occasion to allude to him in his 205th letter, describes him as "a man excelling in learning and wisdom." Sulpitius belonged to an illustrious family. He was very carefully educated, and devoted himself in his early years to the practice of oratory. He acquired a high reputation at the bar; but, while yet in the prime of life, he resolved to leave it, and seek, in company with some pious friends, contentment and peace in a life of retirement and religious exercises. The immediate occasion of this resolution was the premature death of his wife, whom he had married at an early age, and to whom he was deeply attached. His abandonment of the pleasures and pursuits of the world took place about 392 AD; and, notwithstanding all the entreaties and expostulations of his father, he continued, from that date to his death, to lead a life of the strictest seclusion. Becoming a Presbyter of the Church, he attached himself to St. Martin of Tours, for whom he ever afterwards cherished the profoundest admiration and affection, and whose extraordinary career he has traced with a loving pen in by far the most interesting of his works.

It is stated by some ancient writers that Sulpitius ultimately incurred the charge of heresy, having, to some extent, embraced Pelagian opinions. And there has not been a lack of those in modern times who thought they could detect traces of such errors in his works. But it seems to us that there is no ground for any such conclusion. Sulpitius constantly presents himself to us as a most strenuous upholder of "catholic" or "orthodox" doctrines. It is evident that his whole heart was engaged in the love and maintenance of these doctrines: he counts as his "friends" those only who consistently adhered to them; and, while by no means in favor of bitterly prosecuting or severely punishing "heretics," he shrunk with abhorrence from all thought of communion with them. Perhaps the most striking impression we receive from a perusal of his writings is his sincerity. We may often feel that he is over trusting in his acceptance of the miraculous; and we may lament his narrowness in clinging so persistently to mere ecclesiastical formulæ; but we are always impressed with the genuineness of his convictions, and with his fervent desire to bring what he believed to be truth under the attention of his readers.

The style of Sulpitius is, upon the whole, marked by a considerable degree of classical purity and clearness. He has been called "the Christian Sallust," and there are not a few obvious resemblances between the two writers. But some passages occur in Sulpitius which are almost, if not entirely, unintelligible. This is owing partly to the uncertainty of the text, and partly to the use of terms which had sprung up since classical times, and the exact import of which it is impossible to determine. In executing our version of this author (now for the first time, we believe, translated into English), we have had constantly before us the editions of Sigonius (1609), of Hornius (1664), of Vorstius (1709), and of Halm (1866). We have also consulted a very old French translation of the Historia Sacra, published at Rouen in 1580.

The order in which we have arranged the writings of Sulpitius is as follows:—

1. Life of St. Martin.

2. Letters (undoubted).

3. Dialogues.

4. Letters (doubtful).

5. Sacred History.

By far the most attractive of these works are those bearing on the life and achievements of St. Martin. Sulpitius delights to return again and again to this wonderful man, and cannot find language sufficiently strong in which to extol his merits. Hence, not only in the professed Life, but also in the Letters and Dialogues, we have him brought very fully before us. The reader will find near the beginning of the Vita as translated by us, a note bearing upon the solemn asseverations of Sulpitius as to the reality of the miracles which Martin performed.

Most of the Letters here given are deemed spurious by Halm, the latest editor of our author. He has, nevertheless, included the whole of them in his edition, and we have thought it desirable to follow his example in our translation.

The Sacred History of Sulpitius has for its object to present a compendious history of the world from the Creation down to the year 400 AD. The first and longer portion of the work is simply an abridgment of the Scripture narrative. The latter part is more interesting and valuable, as it deals with events lying outside of Scripture, and respecting which we are glad to obtain information from all available sources. Unfortunately, however, Sulpitius is not always a trustworthy authority. His inaccuracies in the first part of his work are very numerous, and will be found pointed out in our version.

The following are some of the Estimates which have been formed of our author. Paulinus, a contemporary of Sulpitius, and bishop of Nola, addressed to him about fifty letters, in the fifth of which he thus writes: "It certainly would not have been given to you to draw up an account of Martin, unless by a pure heart you had rendered your mouth worthy of uttering his sacred praises. You are blessed, therefore, of the Lord, inasmuch as you have been able, in worthy style, and with proper feeling, to complete the history of so great a priest, and so illustrious a confessor. Blessed, too, is he, in accordance with his merits, who has obtained a historian worthy of his faith and of his life; and who has become consecrated to the Divine glory by his own virtues, and to human memory by your narrative regarding him."

Gennadius (died 496 AD), in his "Catalogue of illustrious men," says: "The Presbyter Severus, whose cognomen was Sulpitius, belonged to the province of Aquitania. He was a man distinguished both for his family and learning, and was remarkable for his love of poverty and humility. He was also a great friend of some holy men, such as Martin, bishop of Tours, and Paulinus, bishop of Nola; and his works are by no means to be neglected."

In modern times, J. J. Scaliger has said of Sulpitius, "He is the purest of all the ecclesiastical writers." And Vossius, referring to some remarks of Baronius on Sulpitius, says: "I differ from him (Baronius) in this, that, without sufficient care, he calls Gennadius the contemporary of Severus, since Gennadius flourished seventy years, more or less, after Severus. For he dedicated his book 'On Faith' (as he himself tells us) to Pope Gelasius, who became bishop of Rome in 492 AD. But he greatly extols the holiness of Sulpitius; and in the Roman martyrology his memory (i.e. of Sulpitius) is celebrated on the 29th of January."

Archdeacon Farrar has recently remarked concerning Martin and Sulpitius, "Owing partly to the eloquent and facile style of his (Martin's) biographer, Sulpicius Severus, his name was known from Armenia to Egypt more widely than that of any other monk or bishop of his day."—Lives of the Fathers.

PREFACE TO DESIDERIUS

Severus to his dearest brother Desiderius sends greeting. I had determined, my likeminded brother, to keep private, and confine within the walls of my own house, the little treatise that I had written concerning the life of St. Martin. I did so, as I am not gifted with much talent, and shrank from the criticisms of the world, lest (as I think will be the case) my somewhat unpolished style should displease my readers, and I should be deemed highly worthy of general reprehension for having too boldly laid hold of a subject which ought to have been reserved for truly eloquent writers. But I have not been able to refuse your request again and again presented. For what could there be which I would not grant in deference to your love, even at the expense of my own modesty? However, I have submitted the work to you on the sure understanding that you will reveal it to no other, having received your promise to that effect.

Nevertheless, I have my fears that you will become the means of its publication to the world; and I well know that, once issued, it can never be recalled. If this shall happen, and you come to know that it is read by some others, you will, I trust, kindly ask the readers to attend to the facts related, rather than the language in which they are set forth. You will beg them not to be offended if the style happens unpleasantly to affect their ears, because the kingdom of God consists not of eloquence, but faith.

Let them also bear in mind that salvation was preached to the world, not by orators, but by fishermen, although God could certainly have adopted the other course, had it been advantageous. For my part, indeed, when I first applied my mind to writing what follows, because I thought it disgraceful that the excellences of so great a man should remain concealed, I resolved with myself not to feel ashamed on account of solecisms of language. This I did because I had never attained to any great knowledge of such things; or, if I had formerly some taste of studies of the kind, I had lost the whole of that, through having neglected these matters for so long a course of time. But, after all, that I may not have in future to adopt such an irksome mode of self-defense, the best way will be that the book should be published, if you think right, with the author's name suppressed. In order that this may be done, kindly erase the title that the book bears on its front, so that the page may be silent; and (what is quite enough) let the book proclaim its subject matter, while it tells nothing of the author.

CHAPTER I

REASONS FOR WRITING THE LIFE OF ST. MARTIN

Most men being vainly devoted to the pursuit of worldly glory, have, as they imagined, acquired a memorial of their own names from this source; viz. devoting their pens to the embellishment of the lives of famous men. This course, although it did not secure for them a lasting reputation, still has undoubtedly brought them some fulfilment of the hope they cherished. It has done so, both by preserving their own memory, though to no purpose, and because, through their having presented to the world the examples of great men, no small emulation has been excited in the bosoms of their readers. Yet, notwithstanding these things, their labors have in no degree borne upon the blessed and never-ending life to which we look forward. For what has a glory, destined to perish with the world, profited those men themselves who have written on mere secular matters? Or what benefit has posterity derived from reading of Hector as a warrior, or Socrates as an expounder of philosophy? There can be no profit in such things, since it is not only folly to imitate the persons referred to, but absolute madness not to assail them with the utmost severity.

For, in truth, those persons who estimate human life only by present actions, have consigned their hopes to fables, and their souls to the tomb. In fact, they gave themselves up to be perpetuated simply in the memory of mortals, whereas it is the duty of man rather to seek after eternal life than an eternal memorial and that, not by writing, or fighting, or philosophizing, but by living a pious, holy, and religious life.

This erroneous conduct of mankind, being enshrined in literature, has prevailed to such an extent that it has found many who have been emulous either of the vain philosophy or the foolish excellence which has been celebrated. For this reason, I think I will accomplish something well worth the necessary pains, if I write the life of a most holy man, which shall serve in future as an example to others; by which, indeed, the readers shall be roused to the pursuit of true knowledge, and heavenly warfare, and divine virtue.

In so doing, we have regard also to our own advantage, so that we may look for, not a vain remembrance among men, but an eternal reward from God. For, although we ourselves have not lived in such a manner that we can serve for an example to others, nevertheless, we have made it our endeavor that he should not remain unknown who was a man worthy of imitation.

I shall therefore set about writing the life of St. Martin, and shall narrate both what he did previous to his episcopate, and what he performed as a bishop. At the same time, I cannot hope to set forth all that he was or did. Those excellences of which he alone was conscious are completely unknown, because, as he did not seek for honor from men, he desired, as much as he could accomplish it, that his virtues should be concealed. And even of those which had become known to us, we have omitted a great number, because we have judged it enough if only the more striking and eminent should be recorded.

At the same time, I had in the interests of readers to see to it that, no undue amount of instances being set before them should make them weary of the subject. But I implore those who are to read what follows to give full faith to the things narrated, and to believe that I have written nothing of which I had not certain knowledge and evidence. I should, in fact, have preferred to be silent rather than to narrate things which are false.

CHAPTER II

MILITARY SERVICE OF ST. MARTIN

Martin, then, was born at Sabaria in Pannonia, but was brought up at Ticinum, which is situated in Italy. His parents were, according to the judgment of the world, of no mean rank, but were heathens. His father was at first simply a soldier, but afterwards a military tribune. He himself in his youth following military pursuits was enrolled in the imperial guard, first under king Constantine, and then under Julian Cæsar. This, however, was not done of his own free will, for, almost from his earliest years, the holy infancy of the illustrious boy aspired rather to the service of God. For, when he was of the age of ten years, he betook himself, against the wish of his parents, to the Church, and begged that he might become a catechumen.

Soon afterwards, becoming in a wonderful manner completely devoted to the service of God, when he was twelve years old, he desired to enter on the life of a hermit; and he would have followed up that desire with the necessary vows, had not his as yet too youthful age prevented. His mind, however, being always engaged on matters pertaining to the monasteries or the Church, already meditated in his boyish years what he afterwards, as a professed servant of Christ, fulfilled. But when an edict was issued by the ruling powers in the state, that the sons of veterans should be enrolled for military service, and he, on the information furnished by his father, (who looked with an evil eye on his blessed actions) having been seized and put in chains, when he was fifteen years old, was compelled to take the military oath, then showed himself content with only one servant as his attendant. And even to him, changing places as it were, he often acted as though, while really master, he had been inferior; to such a degree that, for the most part, he drew off his [servant's] boots and cleaned them with his own hand; while they took their meals together, the real master, however, generally acting the part of servant.

During nearly three years before his baptism, he was engaged in the profession of arms, but he kept completely free from those vices in which that class of men become too frequently involved. He showed exceeding kindness towards his fellow-soldiers, and held them in wonderful affection; while his patience and humility surpassed what seemed possible to human nature. There is no need to praise the self-denial which he displayed: it was so great that, even at that date, he was regarded not so much as being a soldier as a monk. By all these qualities he had so endeared himself to the whole body of his comrades, that they esteemed him while they marvellously loved him.

Although not yet made a new creature in Christ, he, by his good works, acted the part of a candidate for baptism. This he did, for instance, by aiding those who were in trouble, by furnishing assistance to the wretched, by supporting the needy, by clothing the naked, while he reserved nothing for himself from his military pay except what was necessary for his daily sustenance. Even then, far from being a senseless hearer of the Gospel, he so far complied with its precepts as to take no thought about tomorrow.

CHAPTER III

CHRIST APPEARS TO ST. MARTIN

Accordingly, at a certain period, when he had nothing except his arms and his simple military dress, in the middle of winter, a winter which had shown itself more severe than ordinary, so that the extreme cold was proving fatal to many, he happened to meet at the gate of the city of Amiens a poor man destitute of clothing. He was entreating those that passed by to have compassion upon him, but all passed the wretched man without notice, when Martin, that man full of God, recognized that a being to whom others showed no pity, was, in that respect, left to him. Yet, what should he do? He had nothing except the cloak in which he was clad, for he had already parted with the rest of his garments for similar purposes.

Taking, therefore, his sword with which he was girt, he divided his cloak into two equal parts, and gave one part to the poor man, while he again clothed himself with the remainder. Upon this, some of the by-standers laughed, because he was now an unsightly object, and stood out as but partly dressed. Many, however, who were of sounder understanding, groaned deeply because they themselves had done nothing similar. They especially felt this, because, being possessed of more than Martin, they could have clothed the poor man without reducing themselves to nakedness.

In the following night, when Martin had resigned himself to sleep, he had a vision of Christ arrayed in that part of his cloak with which he had clothed the poor man. He contemplated the Lord with the greatest attention, and was told to own as his the robe which he had given. Before long, he heard Jesus saying with a clear voice to the multitude of angels standing round—"Martin, who is still but a catechumen, clothed me with this robe." The Lord, truly mindful of his own words (who had said when on earth—"Inasmuch as ye have done these things to one of the least of these, ye have done them unto me), declared that he himself had been clothed in that poor man; and to confirm the testimony he bore to so good a deed, he condescended to show him himself in that very dress which the poor man had received.

After this vision the sainted man was not puffed up with human glory, but, acknowledging the goodness of God in what had been done, and being now of the age of twenty years, he hastened to receive baptism. He did not, however, all at once, retire from military service, yielding to the entreaties of his tribune, whom he admitted to be his familiar tent-companion. For the tribune promised that, after the period of his office had expired, he too would retire from the world. Martin, kept back by the expectation of this event, continued, although but in name, to act the part of a soldier, for nearly two years after he had received baptism.

CHAPTER IV

MARTIN RETIRES FROM MILITARY SERVICE

In the meantime, as the barbarians were rushing within the two divisions of Gaul, Julian Cæsar, bringing an army together at the city of the Vaugiones, began to distribute a donative to the soldiers. As was the custom in such a case, they were called forward, one by one, until it came to the turn of Martin. Then, indeed, judging it a suitable opportunity for seeking his discharge—for he did not think it would be proper for him, if he were not to continue in the service, to receive a donative—he said to Cæsar, "Thus far I have served you as a soldier: allow me now to become a soldier to God: let the man who is to serve you receive your donative:

I am the soldier of Christ: it is not lawful for me to fight."

Then truly the tyrant stormed on hearing such words, declaring that, from fear of the battle, which was to take place the following day, and not from any religious feeling, Martin withdrew from the service. But Martin, full of courage, truly all the more resolute from the danger that had been set before him, exclaims, "If this conduct of mine is ascribed to cowardice, and not to faith, I will take my stand unarmed before the line of battle tomorrow, and in the name of the Lord Jesus, protected by the sign of the cross, and not by shield or helmet, I will safely penetrate the ranks of the enemy."

He is ordered, therefore, to be thrust back into prison, determined on proving his words true by exposing himself unarmed to the barbarians. But, on the following day, the enemy sent ambassadors to treat about peace and surrendered both themselves and all their possessions. In these circumstances who can doubt that this victory was due to the saintly man? It was granted him that he should not be sent unarmed to the fight. And although the good Lord could have preserved his own soldier, even amid the swords and darts of the enemy, yet that his blessed eyes might not be pained by witnessing the death of others, he removed all necessity for fighting. For Christ did not require to secure any other victory in behalf of his own soldier, than that, the enemy being subdued without bloodshed, no one should suffer death.

CHAPTER V

MARTIN CONVERTS A ROBBER TO THE FAITH

From that time quitting military service, Martin earnestly sought after the society of Hilarius, bishop of the city Pictava, whose faith in the things of God was then regarded as of high renown, and in universal esteem. For some time Martin made his abode with him. Now, this same Hilarius, having instituted him in the office of the diaconate, endeavored still more closely to attach him to himself, and to bind him by leading him to take part in Divine service.

But when he constantly refused, crying out that he was unworthy, Hilarius, as being a man of deep penetration, perceived that he could only be constrained in this way, if he should lay that sort of office upon him, in discharging which there should seem to be a kind of injury done him. He therefore appointed him to be an exorcist. Martin did not refuse this appointment, from the fear that he might seem to have looked down upon it as somewhat humble. Not long after this, he was warned in a dream that he should visit his native land, and more particularly his parents, who were still involved in heathenism, with a regard for their religious interests.

He set forth in accordance with the expressed wish of the holy Hilarius, and, after being adjured by him with many prayers and tears, that he would in due time return. According to report Martin entered on that journey in a melancholy frame of mind, after calling the brethren to witness that many sufferings lay before him. The result fully justified this prediction.

For, first of all, having followed some devious paths among the Alps, he fell into the hands of robbers. And when one of them lifted up his axe and poised it above Martin's head, another of them met with his right hand the blow as it fell; nevertheless, having had his hands bound behind his back, he was handed over to one of them to be guarded and stripped. The robber, having led him to a private place apart from the rest, began to enquire of him who he was. Upon this, Martin replied that he was a Christian. The robber next asked him whether he was afraid. Then indeed Martin most courageously replied that he never before had felt so safe, because he knew that the mercy of the Lord would be especially present with him in the midst of trials. He added that he grieved rather for the man in whose hands he was, because, by living a life of robbery, he was showing himself unworthy of the mercy of Christ.

And then entering on a discourse concerning Evangelical truth, he preached the word of God to the robber. Why should I delay stating the result? The robber believed; and, after expressing his respect for Martin, he restored him to the way, entreating him to pray the Lord for him. That same robber was afterwards seen leading a religious life; so that, in fact, the narrative I have given above is based upon an account furnished by himself.

CHAPTER VI

THE DEVIL THROWS HIMSELF IN THE WAY OF MARTIN

Martin, then, having gone on from there, after he had passed Milan, the devil met him in the way, having assumed the form of a man. The devil first asked him to what place he was going. Martin having answered him to the effect that he was minded to go wherever the Lord called him, the devil said to him, "Wherever you go, or whatever you attempt, the devil will resist you." Then Martin, replying to him in the prophetical word, said, "The Lord is my helper; I will not fear what man can do to me." Upon this, his enemy immediately vanished out of his sight; and thus, as he had intended in his heart and mind, he set free his mother from the errors of heathenism, though his father continued to cleave to its evils.

However, he saved many by his example. After this, when the Arian heresy had spread through the whole world, and was especially powerful in Illyria, and when he, almost single-handed, was fighting most strenuously against the treachery of the priests, and had been subjected to many punishments (for he was publicly scourged, and at last was compelled to leave the city), again betaking himself to Italy, and having found the Church in the two divisions of Gaul in a distracted condition through the departure also of the holy Hilarius, whom the violence of the heretics had driven into exile, he established a monastery for himself at Milan.

There, too, Auxentius, the originator and leader of the Arians, bitterly persecuted him; and, after he had assailed him with many injuries, violently expelled him from the city. Thinking, therefore, that it was necessary to yield to circumstances, he withdrew to the island Gallinaria, with a certain presbyter as his companion, a man of distinguished excellences.

Here he subsisted for some time on the roots of plants; and, while doing so, he ate hellebore, which is, as people say, a poisonous kind of grass. But when he perceived the strength of the poison increasing within him, and death now nearly at hand, he warded off the imminent danger by means of prayer, and immediately all his pains were put to flight. And not long after having discovered that, through penitence on the part of the king, permission to return had been granted to holy Hilarius, he made an effort to meet him at Rome, and, with this view, set out for that city.

CHAPTER VII

MARTIN RESTORES A CATECHUMEN TO LIFE

As Hilarius had already gone away, so Martin followed in his footsteps; and having been most joyously welcomed by him, he established for himself a monastery not far from the town. At this time a certain catechumen joined him, being desirous of becoming instructed in the doctrines and habits of the most holy man. But, after the lapse only of a few days, the catechumen, seized with a languor, began to suffer from a violent fever.

It so happened that Martin had then left home, and having remained away three days, he found on his return that life had departed from the catechumen; and so suddenly had death occurred, that he had left this world without receiving baptism. The body being laid out in public was being honored by the last sad offices on the part of the mourning brethren, when Martin hurries up to them with tears and lamentations. But then laying hold, as it were, of the Holy Spirit, with the whole powers of his mind, he orders the others to leave the cell in which the body was lying; and bolting the door, he stretches himself at full length on the dead limbs of the departed brother.

Having given himself for some time to earnest prayer, and perceiving by means of the Spirit of God that power was present, he then rose up for a little, and gazing on the countenance of the deceased, he waited without misgiving for the result of his prayer and of the mercy of the Lord. And scarcely had the space of two hours elapsed, when he saw the dead man begin to move a little in all his members, and to tremble with his eyes opened for the practice of sight.

Then indeed, turning to the Lord with a loud voice and giving thanks, he filled the cell with his outbursts of praise. Hearing the noise, those who had been standing at the door immediately rush inside. And truly a marvelous spectacle met them, for they beheld the man alive whom they had formerly left dead. Thus being restored to life, and having immediately obtained baptism, he lived for many years afterwards; and he was the first who offered himself to us both as a subject that had experienced the virtues of Martin, and as a witness to their existence.

The same man was inclined to relate that, when he left the body, he was brought before the tribunal of the Judge, and being assigned to gloomy regions and vulgar crowds, he received a severe sentence. Then, however, he added, it was suggested by two angels of the Judge that he was the man for whom Martin was praying; and that, on this account, he was ordered to be led back by the same angels, and given up to Martin, and restored to his former life. From this time forward, the name of the sainted man became illustrious, so that, as being reckoned holy by all, he was also deemed powerful and truly apostolical.

CHAPTER VIII

MARTIN RESTORES ONE THAT HAD BEEN STRANGLED

Not long after these events, while Martin was passing by the estate of a certain man named Lupicinus, who was held in high esteem according to the judgment of the world, he was received with shouting and the lamentations of a wailing crowd. Having, in an anxious state of mind gone up to that multitude, and enquired what such weeping meant, he was told that one of the slaves of the family had put an end to his life by hanging.

Hearing this, Martin entered the cell in which the body was lying, and, excluding the entire multitude, he stretched himself upon the body, and spent some little time in prayer. Before long, the deceased, with life beaming in his countenance, and with his drooping eyes fixed on Martin's face, is aroused; and with a gentle effort attempting to rise, he laid hold of the right hand of the saintly man, and by this means stood upon his feet. In this manner, while the whole multitude looked on, he walked along with Martin to the porch of the house.

CHAPTER IX

High Esteem in which Martin was held

Nearly about the same time, Martin was called upon to undertake the episcopate of the church at Tours; but when he could not easily be drawn forth from his monastery, a certain Ruricius, one of the citizens, pretending that his wife was ill, and casting himself down at his knees, prevailed on him to go forth. Multitudes of the citizens having previously been posted by the road on which he traveled, he is thus under a kind of guard escorted to the city. An incredible number of people not only from that town, but also from the neighboring cities, had, in a wonderful manner, assembled to give their votes.

There was but one wish among all, there were the same

prayers, and there was the same fixed opinion to the effect that Martin was most worthy of the episcopate, and that the church would be happy with such a priest. A few persons, however, and among these some of the bishops, who had been summoned to appoint a chief priest, were impiously offering resistance, asserting that Martin's person was contemptible, that he was unworthy of the episcopate, that he was a man despicable in countenance, that his clothing was shameful, and his hair disgusting. This madness of theirs was ridiculed by the people of sounder judgment, inasmuch as such objectors only proclaimed the illustrious character of the man, while they sought to slander him. Nor truly was it allowed them to do anything else, than what the people, following the Divine will, desired to be accomplished.

Among the bishops, however, who had been present, a certain one of the name Defensor is said to have specially offered opposition; and on this account it was observed that he was at the time severely censured in the reading from the prophets. For when it so happened that the reader, whose duty it was to read in public that day, being blocked out by the people, failed to appear, the officials falling into confusion, while they waited for him who never came, one of those standing by, laying hold of the Psalter, seized upon the first verse which presented itself to him.

Now, the Psalm ran thus: "Out of the mouth of babes and sucklings You have perfected praise because of Your enemies, that You may destroy the enemy and the avenger." On these words being read, a shout was raised by the people, and the opposite party were confounded. It was believed that this Psalm had been chosen by Divine ordination, that Defensor might hear a testimony to his own work, because the praise of the Lord was perfected out of the mouth of babes and sucklings in the case of Martin, while the enemy was at the same time both pointed out and destroyed.

CHAPTER X

MARTIN AS BISHOP OF TOURS

And now having entered on the episcopal office, it is beyond my power fully to set forth how Martin distinguished himself in the discharge of its duties. For he remained with the utmost constancy, the same as he had been before. There was the same humility in his heart, and the same homeliness in his garments. Full alike of dignity and courtesy, he kept up the position of a bishop properly, yet in such a way as not to lay aside the objects and virtues of a monk.

Accordingly he made use, for some time, of the cell connected with the church; but afterwards, when he felt it impossible to tolerate the disturbance caused by the numbers of those visiting it, he established a monastery for himself about two miles outside the city. This spot was so secret and retired that he enjoyed in it the solitude of a hermit. For, on one side, it was surrounded by a precipitous rock of a lofty mountain, while the river Loire had shut in the rest of the plain by a bay extending back for a little distance; and the place could be approached only by one, and that a very narrow passage. Here, then, he possessed a cell constructed of wood. Many also of the brethren had, in the same manner, fashioned retreats for themselves, but most of them had formed these out of the rock of the overhanging mountain, hollowed into caves.

There were altogether eighty disciples, who were being disciplined after the example of the saintly master. No one there had anything which was called his own; all things were possessed in common. It was not allowed either to buy or to sell anything, as is the custom among most monks. No art was practiced there, except that of transcribers, and even this was assigned to the brethren of younger years, while the elders spent their time in prayer.

Rarely did any one of them go beyond the cell, unless when they assembled at the place of prayer. They all took their food together, after the hour of fasting was past. No one used wine, except when illness compelled them to do so. Most of them were clothed in garments of camels' hair. Any dress approaching to softness was there deemed criminal, and this must be thought the more remarkable, because many among them were such as are deemed of noble rank. These, though far differently brought up, had forced themselves down to this degree of humility and patient endurance, and we have seen numbers of these afterwards made bishops. For what city or church would there be that would not desire to have its priests from among those in the monastery of Martin?

CHAPTER XI

MARTIN DEMOLISHES AN ALTAR CONSECRATED TO A ROBBER

But let me proceed to a description of other excellences which Martin displayed as a bishop. There was, not far from the town, a place very close to the monastery, which a false human opinion had consecrated, on the supposition that some martyrs had been buried together there. For it was also believed that an altar had been placed there by former bishops.

But Martin, not inclined to give a hasty belief to things uncertain, often asked from those who were his elders, whether among the presbyters or clerics, that the name of the martyr, or the time when he suffered, should be made known to him. He did so, he said, because he had great scruples on these points, inasmuch as no steady tradition respecting them had come down from antiquity. Having, therefore, for a time kept away from the place, by no means wishing to lessen the religious veneration with which it was regarded, because he was as yet uncertain, but, at the same time not lending his authority to the opinion of the multitude, lest a mere superstition should obtain a firmer footing, he one day went out to the place, taking a few brethren with him as companions.

There standing above the very tomb, Martin prayed to the Lord that he would reveal, who the man in question was, and what was his character or desert. Next turning to the left-hand side, he sees standing very near a shade of a mean and cruel appearance. Martin commands him to tell his name and character. Upon this, he declares his name, and confesses his guilt. He says that he had been a robber, and that he was beheaded on account of his crimes; that he had been honored simply by an error of the multitude; that he had nothing in common with the martyrs, since glory was their portion, while punishment exacted its penalties from him. Those who stood by heard, in a wonderful way, the voice of the speaker, but they beheld no person. Then Martin made known what he had seen, and ordered the altar that had been there to be removed, and thus he delivered the people from the error of that superstition.

CHAPTER XII

MARTIN CAUSES THE BEARERS OF A DEAD BODY TO STOP

Now, it came to pass some time after the above, that while Martin was going a journey, he met the body of a certain heathen, which was being carried to the tomb with superstitious funeral rites. Perceiving from a distance the crowd that was approaching, and being ignorant as to what was going on, he stood still for a little while. For there was a distance of nearly half a mile between him and the crowd, so that it was difficult to discover what the spectacle he beheld really was.

Nevertheless, because he saw it was a rustic gathering, and when the linen clothes spread over the body were blown about by the action of the wind, he believed that some profane rites of sacrifice were being performed. This thought occurred to him, because it was the custom of the Gallic rustics in their wretched folly to carry about through the fields the images of demons veiled with a white covering.

Lifting up, therefore, the sign of the cross opposite to them, he commanded the crowd not to move from the place in which they were, and to set down the burden. Upon this, the miserable creatures might have been seen at first to become stiff like rocks. Next, as they endeavored, with every possible effort, to move forward, but were not able to take a step farther, they began to whirl themselves about in the most ridiculous fashion, until, not able any longer to sustain the weight, they set down the dead body.

Thunderstruck, and gazing in bewilderment at each other as not knowing what had happened to them they remained sunk in silent thought. But when the saintly man discovered that they were simply a band of peasants celebrating funeral rites, and not sacrifices to the gods, again raising his hand, he gave them the power of going away, and of lifting up the body. Thus he both compelled them to stand when he pleased, and permitted them to depart when he thought good.

CHAPTER XIII

MARTIN ESCAPES FROM A FALLING PINE-TREE

Again, when in a certain village he had demolished a very ancient temple, and had set about cutting down a pine-tree, which stood close to the temple, the chief priest of that place, and a crowd of other heathens began to oppose him. And these people, though, under the influence of the Lord, they had been quiet while the temple was being overthrown, could not patiently allow the tree to be cut down.

Martin carefully instructed them that there was nothing sacred in the trunk of a tree, and urged them rather to honor God whom he himself served. He added that there was a moral necessity why that tree should be cut down, because it had been dedicated to a demon. Then one of them who was bolder than the others says, "If you have any trust in thy God, whom you say you worship, we ourselves will cut down this tree, and be it your part to receive it when falling; for if, as you declare, your Lord is with you, you will escape all injury."

Then Martin, courageously trusting in the Lord, promises that he would do what had been asked. Upon this, all that crowd of heathen agreed to the condition named; for they held the loss of their tree a small matter, if only they got the enemy of their religion buried beneath its fall. Accordingly, since that pine-tree was hanging over in one direction, so that there was no doubt to what side it would fall on being cut, Martin, having been bound, is, in accordance with the decision of these pagans, placed in that spot where, as no one doubted, the tree was about to fall.

They began, therefore, to cut down their own tree, with great glee and joyfulness, while there was at some distance a great multitude of wondering spectators. And now the pine-tree began to totter, and to threaten its[1] own ruin by falling. The monks at a distance grew pale, and, terrified by the danger ever coming nearer, had lost all hope and

1   Perhaps "suam" here stands for "ejus," as in other passages of our author. The meaning will then be, "and to threaten his (Martin's) destruction by falling."

confidence, expecting only the death of Martin. But he, trusting in the Lord, and waiting courageously, when now the falling pine had uttered its expiring crash, while it was now falling, while it was just rushing upon him, simply holding up his hand against it, he put in its way the sign of salvation.

Then, indeed, after the manner of a spinning-top (one might have thought it driven back), it swept round to the opposite side, to such a degree that it almost crushed the rustics, who had taken their places there in what was deemed a safe spot. Then truly, a shout being raised to heaven, the heathen were amazed by the miracle, while the monks wept for joy; and the name of Christ was praised by all. The well-known result was that on that day salvation came to that region. For there was hardly one of that immense multitude of heathens who did not express a desire for the imposition of hands, and abandoning his impious errors, made a profession of faith in the Lord Jesus.

Certainly, before the times of Martin, very few, indeed, almost none, in those regions had received the name of Christ; but through his virtues and example that name has prevailed to such an extent, that now there is no place around there which is not filled either with very crowded churches or monasteries. For wherever he destroyed heathen temples, there he used immediately to build either churches or monasteries.

CHAPTER XIV

MARTIN DESTROYS HEATHEN TEMPLES AND ALTARS

Nor did he show less eminence, much about the same time, in other transactions of a like kind. For, having in a certain village set fire to a very ancient and celebrated temple, the circle of flames was carried by the action of the wind upon a house which was very close to, indeed, connected with, the temple. When Martin perceived this, he climbed by rapid ascent to the roof of the house, presenting himself in front of the advancing flames. Then indeed might the fire have been seen thrust back in a wonderful manner against the force of the wind, so that there appeared a sort of conflict of the two elements fighting together. Thus, by the influence of Martin, the fire only acted in the place where it was ordered to do so.

But in a village which was named Leprosum, when he too wished to overthrow a temple which had acquired great wealth through the superstitious ideas entertained of its sanctity, a multitude of the heathen resisted him to such a degree that he was driven back not without bodily injury. He, therefore, withdrew to a place in the vicinity, and there for three days, clothed in sackcloth and ashes fasting and praying the whole time, he besought the Lord, that, as he had not been able to overthrow that temple by human effort, Divine power might be exerted to destroy it. Then two angels, with spears and shields after the manner of heavenly warriors, suddenly presented themselves to him, saying that they were sent by the Lord to put to flight the rustic multitude, and to furnish protection to Martin, lest, while the temple was being destroyed, any one should offer resistance.

They told him therefore to return, and complete the blessed work that he had begun. Accordingly Martin returned to the village; and while the crowds of heathen looked on in perfect quiet as he demolished the pagan temple even to the foundations, he also reduced all the altars and images to dust. At this sight the rustics, when they perceived that they had been so astounded and terrified by an intervention of the Divine will, that they might not be found fighting against the bishop, almost all believed in the

Lord Jesus. They then began to cry out openly and to confess that the God of Martin ought to be worshiped, and that the idols should be despised, which were not able to help them.

CHAPTER XV

MARTIN OFFERS HIS NECK TO AN ASSASSIN

I shall also relate what took place in the village of the Ædui. When Martin was there overthrowing a temple, a multitude of rustic heathen rushed upon him in a frenzy of rage. And when one of them, bolder than the rest, made an attack upon him with a drawn sword, Martin, throwing back his cloak, offered his bare neck to the assassin. Nor did the heathen delay to strike, but in the very act of lifting up his right arm, he fell to the ground on his back, and being overwhelmed by the fear of God, he entreated for pardon. Not unlike this was that other event which happened to Martin, that when a certain man had resolved to wound him with a knife as he was destroying some idols, at the very moment of fetching the blow, the weapon was struck out of his hands and disappeared.

Very frequently, too, when the pagans were addressing him to the effect that he would not overthrow their temples, he so soothed and conciliated the minds of the heathen by his holy discourse that, the light of truth having been revealed to them, they themselves overthrew their own temples.

CHAPTER XVI

CURES EFFECTED BY ST. MARTIN

Moreover, the gift of accomplishing cures was so largely possessed by Martin, that scarcely any sick person came to him for assistance without being at once restored to health. This will clearly appear from the following example.

A certain girl at Treves was so completely prostrated by a terrible paralysis that for a long time she had been quite unable to make use of her body for any purpose, and being, as it were, already dead, only the smallest breath of life seemed still to remain in her. Her afflicted relatives were standing by, expecting nothing but her death, when it was suddenly announced that Martin had come to that city. When the father of the girl found that such was the case, he ran to make a request in behalf of his all but lifeless child.

It happened that Martin had already entered the church. There, while the people were looking on, and in the presence of many other bishops, the old man, uttering a cry of grief, embraced the saint's knees and said: "My daughter is dying of a miserable kind of infirmity; and, what is more dreadful than death itself, she is now alive only in the spirit, her flesh being already dead before the time. I beseech thee to go to her, and give her thy blessing; for I believe that through you she will be restored to health." Martin, troubled by such an address, was bewildered, and shrank back, saying that this was a matter not in his own hands; that the old man was mistaken in the judgment he had formed; and that he was not worthy to be the instrument through whom the Lord should make a display of his power.

The father, in tears, persevered in still more earnestly pressing the case, and entreated Martin to visit the dying girl. At last, constrained by the bishops standing by to go as requested, he went down to the home of the girl. An immense crowd was waiting at the doors, to see what the servant of the Lord would do. And first, betaking himself to his familiar arms in affairs of that kind, he cast himself down on the ground and prayed. Then gazing earnestly upon the ailing girl, he requests that oil should be given him. After he had received and blessed this, he poured the powerful sacred liquid into the mouth of the girl, and immediately her voice returned to her. Then gradually, through contact with him, her limbs began, one by one, to recover life, till, at last, in the presence of the people, she arose with firm steps.

CHAPTER XVII

MARTIN CASTS OUT SEVERAL DEVILS

At the same time the servant of one Tetradius, a man of proconsular rank, having been laid hold of by a demon, was tormented with the most miserable results. Martin, therefore, having been asked to lay his hands on him, ordered the servant to be brought to him; but the evil spirit could, in no way, be brought forth from the cell in which he was: he showed himself so fearful, with ferocious teeth, to those who attempted to draw near.

Then Tetradius throws himself at the feet of the saintly man, imploring that he himself would go down to the house in which the possessed of the devil was kept. But

Martin then declared that he could not visit the house of an unconverted heathen. For Tetradius, at that time, was still involved in the errors of heathenism. He, therefore, pledges his word that if the demon were driven out of the boy, he would become a Christian. Martin, then, laying his hand upon the boy, cast the evil spirit out of him. On seeing this, Tetradius believed in the Lord Jesus, and immediately became a catechumen, while, not long after, he was baptized; and he always regarded Martin with extraordinary affection, as having been the author of his salvation.

About the same time, having entered the dwelling of a certain householder in the same town, he stopped short at the very threshold, and said, that he perceived a horrible demon in the courtyard of the house. When Martin ordered it to depart, it laid hold of a certain member of the family, who was staying in the inner part of the house; and the poor wretch began at once to rage with his teeth, and to lacerate whomever he met. The house was thrown into disorder; the family was in confusion; and the people present took to flight.

Martin threw himself in the way of the frenzied creature, and first of all commanded him to stand still. But when he continued to gnash with his teeth, and, with gaping mouth, was threatening to bite, Martin inserted his fingers into his mouth, and said, "If you possess any power, devour these." But then, as if red-hot iron had entered his jaws, drawing his teeth far away he took care not to touch the fingers of the saintly man; and when he was compelled by punishments and tortures, to flee out of the possessed body, while he had no power of escaping by the mouth, he was cast out by means of a defluxion of the belly, leaving disgusting traces behind him.

CHAPTER XVIII

MARTIN PERFORMS
VARIOUS MIRACLES

In the meanwhile, as a sudden report had troubled the city as to the movement and inroad of the barbarians, Martin orders a possessed person to be set before him, and commanded him to declare whether this message was true or not. Then he confessed that there were sixteen demons who had spread this report among the people, in order that by the fear thus excited, Martin might have to flee from the city, but that, in fact, nothing was less in the minds of the barbarians than to make any inroad. When the unclean spirit thus acknowledged these things in the midst of the church, the city was set free from the fear and tumult which had at the time been felt.

At Paris, again, when Martin was entering the gate of the city, with large crowds attending him, he gave a kiss to a leper, of miserable appearance, while all shuddered at seeing him do so; and Martin blessed him, with the result that he was instantly cleansed from all his misery. On the following day, the man appearing in the church with a healthy skin, gave thanks for the soundness of body which he had recovered. This fact, too, ought not to be passed over in silence, that threads from Martin's garment, or such as had been plucked from the sackcloth which he wore, wrought frequent miracles upon those who were sick. For, by either being tied round the fingers or placed about the neck, they very often drove away diseases from the afflicted.

CHAPTER XIX

A LETTER OF MARTIN EFFECTS A CURE, WITH OTHER MIRACLES

Further, Arborius, an ex-prefect, and a man of a very holy and faithful character, while his daughter was in agony from the burning fever of a quartan ague, inserted in the bosom of the girl, at the very paroxysm of the heat, a letter of Martin which happened to have been brought to him, and immediately the fever was dispelled. This event had such an influence upon Arborius, that he at once consecrated the girl to God, and devoted her to perpetual virginity. Then, proceeding to Martin, he presented the girl to him, as an obvious living example of his power of working miracles, inasmuch as she had been cured by him though absent; and he would not suffer her to be consecrated by any other than Martin, through his placing upon her the dress characteristic of virginity.

Paulinus, too, a man who was afterwards to furnish a striking example of the age, having begun to suffer grievously in one of his eyes, and when a pretty thick skin having grown over it had already covered up its pupil, Martin touched his eye with a painter's brush, and, all pain being removed, thus restored it to its former soundness. He himself also, when, by a certain accident, he had fallen out of an upper room, and tumbling down a broken, uneven stair, had received many wounds, as he lay in his cell at the point of death, and was tortured with grievous sufferings, saw in the night an angel appear to him, who washed his wounds, and applied healing ointment to the bruised members of his body.

As the effect of this, he found himself on the morrow restored to soundness of health, so that he was not thought to have suffered any harm. But because it would be tedious to go through everything of this kind, let these examples suffice, as a few out of a multitude; and let it be enough that we do not in striking cases [of miraculous interposition] detract from the truth, while, having so many to choose from, we avoid exciting weariness in the reader.

CHAPTER XX

HOW MARTIN ACTED TOWARDS THE EMPEROR MAXIMUS

And here to insert some smaller matters among things so great (although such is the nature of our times in which all things have fallen into decay and corruption, it is almost a pre-eminent virtue for priestly firmness not to have yielded to royal flattery), when a number of bishops from various parts had assembled to the Emperor Maximus, a man of fierce character, and at that time elated with the victory he had won in the civil wars, and when the disgraceful flattery of all around the emperor was generally remarked, while the priestly dignity had, with degenerate submissiveness, taken a second place to the royal retinue, in Martin alone, apostolic authority continued to assert itself.

For even if he had to make suit to the sovereign for some things, he commanded rather than entreated him; and although often invited, he kept away from his entertainments, saying that he could not take a place at the table of one who, out of two emperors, had deprived one of his kingdom, and the other of his life.

At last, when Maximus maintained that he had not of his own accord assumed the sovereignty, but that he had simply defended by arms the necessary requirements of the empire, regard to which had been imposed upon him by the soldiers, according to the Divine appointment, and that the favor of God did not seem wanting to him who, by an event seemingly so incredible, had secured the victory, adding to that the statement that none of his adversaries had been slain except in the open field of battle, at length, Martin, overcome either by his reasoning or his entreaties, came to the royal banquet.

The king was wonderfully pleased because he had gained this point. Moreover, there were guests present who had been invited as if to a festival; men of the highest and most illustrious rank,—the prefect, who was also consul, named Evodius, one of the most righteous men that ever lived; two courtiers possessed of the greatest power, the brother and uncle of the king, while between these two, the presbyter of

Martin had taken his place; but he himself occupied a seat which was set quite close to the king. About the middle of the banquet, according to custom, one of the servants presented a goblet to the king. He orders it rather to be given to the very holy bishop, expecting and hoping that he should then receive the cup from his right hand. But Martin, when he had drunk, handed the goblet to his own presbyter, as thinking no one worthier to drink next to himself, and holding that it would not be right for him to prefer either the king himself, or those who were next the king, to the presbyter. And the emperor, as well as all those who were then present, admired this conduct so much, that this very thing, by which they had been undervalued, gave them pleasure.

The report then ran through the whole palace that Martin had done, at the king's dinner, what no bishop had dared to do at the banquets of the lowest judges. And Martin predicted to the same Maximus long before, that if he went into Italy to which he then desired to go, waging war, against the Emperor Valentinianus, it would come to pass that he should know he would[2] indeed be victorious in the first attack, but would perish a short time afterwards. And we have seen that this did in fact take place. For, on his first arrival Valentinianus had to betake himself to flight but

---

2   There is considerable confusion in this sentence.

recovering his strength about a year afterwards, Maximus was taken and slain by him within the walls of Aquileia.

CHAPTER XXI

MARTIN HAS TO DO BOTH WITH ANGELS AND DEVILS

It is also well known that angels were very often seen by him, so that they spoke in turns with him in set speech. As to the devil, Martin held him so visible and ever under the power of his eyes, that whether he kept himself in his proper form, or changed himself into different shapes of spiritual wickedness, he was perceived by Martin, under whatever guise he appeared. The devil knew well that he could not escape discovery, and therefore frequently heaped insults upon Martin, being unable to beguile him by trickery.

On one occasion the devil, holding in his hand the bloody horn of an ox, rushed into Martin's cell with great noise, and holding out to him his bloody right hand, while at the same time he exulted in the crime he had committed, said: "Where, O Martin, is thy power? I have just slain one of your people." Then Martin assembled the brethren, and related to them what the devil had disclosed, while he ordered them carefully to search the several cells in order to discover who had been visited with this calamity. They report that no one of the monks was missing, but that one peasant, hired by them, had gone to the forest to bring home wood in his wagon.

Upon hearing this, Martin instructs some of them to go and meet him. On their doing so, the man was found almost dead at no great distance from the monastery. Nevertheless, although just drawing his last breath, he made known to the brethren the cause of his wound and death. He said that, while he was drawing tighter the thongs which had got loose on the oxen yoked together, one of the oxen, throwing his head free, had wounded him with his horn in the groin. And not long after the man died. You see with what judgment of the Lord this power was given to the devil. This was a marvelous feature in Martin that not only on this occasion to which I have specially referred, but on many occasions of the same kind, in fact as often as such things occurred, he perceived them long beforehand, and disclosed the things which had been revealed to him to the brethren.

CHAPTER XXII

MARTIN PREACHES REPENTANCE EVEN TO THE DEVIL

Now, the devil, while he tried to impose upon the holy man by a thousand injurious arts, often thrust himself upon him in a visible form, but in very various shapes. For sometimes he presented himself to his view changed into the person of Jupiter, often into that of Mercury and Minerva. Often, too, were heard words of reproach, in which the crowd of demons assailed Martin with scurrilous expressions. But knowing that all were false and groundless, he was not affected by the charges brought against him.

Moreover, some of the brethren bore witness that they had heard a demon reproaching Martin in abusive terms, and asking why he had taken back, on their subsequent repentance, certain of the brethren who had, some time previously, lost their baptism by falling into various errors. The demon set forth the crimes of each of them; but they added that Martin, resisting the devil firmly, answered him, that by-past sins are cleansed away by the leading of a better life, and that through the mercy of God, those are to be absolved from their sins who have given up their evil ways. The devil saying in opposition to this that such guilty men as those referred to did not come within the pale of pardon, and that no mercy was extended by the Lord to those who had once fallen away,

Martin is said to have cried out in words to the following effect: "If you, yourself, wretched being, would but desist from attacking mankind, and even, at this period, when the day of judgment is at hand, would only repent of your deeds, I, with a true confidence in the Lord, would promise you the mercy of Christ."[3]

---

3   This is a truly noteworthy passage. It anticipates a well-known sentiment of Burns, the national bard of Scotland. In his Address to the Deil, Burns has said that if the great enemy would only "tak a thocht an' men'," he might still have a chance of safety, and this idea seems very much in accordance with the opinion of St. Martin as expressed above. Hornius, however, is very indignant on account of it, and exclaims: "Intolerabilis hic Martini error. Nec Sulpicius excusatione sua demit, sed auget. Origenes primus ejus er-

O what a holy boldness with respect to the loving-kindness of the Lord, in which, although he could not assert authority, he nevertheless showed the feelings dwelling within him! And since our discourse has here sprung up concerning the devil and his devices, it does not seem away from the point, although the matter does not bear immediately upon Martin, to relate what took place; both because the virtues of Martin do, to some extent, appear in the transaction, and the incident, which was worthy of a miracle, will properly be put on record, with the view of furnishing a caution, should anything of a similar character subsequently occur.

roris author."

CHAPTER XXIII

A Case of Diabolic Deception

There was a certain man, Clarus by name, a most noble youth, who afterwards became a presbyter, and who is now, through his happy departure from this world, numbered among the saints. He, leaving all others, betook himself to Martin, and in a short time became distinguished for the most exalted faith, and for all sorts of excellence. Now, it came to pass that, when he had erected an abode for himself not far from the monastery of the bishop, and many brethren were staying with him, a certain youth, Anatolius by name, having, under the profession of a monk, falsely assumed every appearance of humility and innocence, came to him, and lived for some time on the common store along with the rest.

Then, as time went on, he began to affirm that angels were in the habit of talking with him. As no one gave any credit to his words, he urged a number of the brethren to believe by certain signs. At length he went to such a length as to declare that angels passed between him and God; and now he wished that he should be regarded as one of the prophets. Clarus, however, could by no means be induced to believe. He then began to threaten Clarus with the anger of God and present afflictions, because he did not believe one of the saints. At the last, he is related to have burst forth with the following declaration: "Behold, the Lord will this night give me a white robe out of heaven, clothed in which, I will dwell in the midst of you; and that will be to you a sign that I am the Power of God, inasmuch as I have been presented with the garment of God." Then truly the expectation of all was highly raised by this profession.

Accordingly, about the middle of the night, it was seen, by the noise of people moving eagerly about, that the whole monastery in the place was excited. It might be seen, too, that the cell in which the young man referred to lived was glittering with numerous lights; and the whisperings of those moving about in it, as well as a kind of murmur of many voices, could be heard. Then, on silence being secured, the youth coming forth calls one of the brethren, Sabatius by name, to himself, and shows him the robe in which he had been clothed. He again, filled with amazement, gathers the rest together, and Clarus himself also runs up; and a light being obtained, they all carefully inspect the garment. Now, it was of the utmost softness, of marvelous brightness, and of glittering purple, and yet no one could discover what was its nature, or of what sort of fleece it had been formed. However, when it was more minutely examined by the eyes or fingers, it seemed nothing else than a garment.

In the meantime, Clarus urges upon the brethren to be earnest in prayer, that the Lord would show them more clearly what it really was. Accordingly, the rest of the night was spent in singing hymns and psalms. But when day broke, Clarus wished to take the young man by the hand, and bring him to Martin, being well aware that he could not be deceived by any arts of the devil. Then, indeed, the miserable man began to resist and refuse, and affirmed that he had been forbidden to show himself to Martin. And when they compelled him to go against his will, the garment vanished from among the hands of those who were conducting him. Wherefore, who can doubt that this, too, was an illustration of the power of Martin, so that the devil could no longer dissemble or conceal his own deception, when it was to be submitted to the eyes of Martin?

CHAPTER XXIV

MARTIN IS TEMPTED BY THE WILES OF THE DEVIL

It was found, again, that about the same time there was a young man in Spain, who, having by many signs obtained for himself authority among the people, was puffed up to such a pitch that he gave himself out as being Elias. And when multitudes had too readily believed this, he went on to say that he was actually Christ; and he succeeded so well even in this delusion that a certain bishop named Rufus worshiped him as being the Lord. For so doing, we have seen this bishop at a later date deprived of his office.

Many of the brethren have also informed me that at the same time one arose in the East, who boasted that he was

John. We may infer from this, since false prophets of such a kind have appeared, that the coming of Antichrist is at hand; for he is already practicing in these persons the mystery of iniquity. And truly I think this point should not be passed over, with what arts the devil about this very time tempted Martin.

For, on a certain day, prayer having been previously offered, and the fiend himself being surrounded by a purple light, in order that he might the more easily deceive people by the brilliance of the splendor assumed, clothed also in a royal robe, and with a crown of precious stones and gold encircling his head, his shoes too being inlaid with gold, while he presented a tranquil countenance, and a generally rejoicing aspect, so that no such thought as that he was the devil might be entertained—he stood by the side of Martin as he was praying in his cell.

The saint being dazzled by his first appearance, both preserved a long and deep silence. This was first broken by the devil, who said: "Acknowledge, Martin, who it is that you behold. I am Christ; and being just about to descend to earth, I wished first to manifest myself to you." When Martin kept silence on hearing these words, and gave no answer whatever, the devil dared to repeat his audacious declaration: "Martin, why do you hesitate to believe, when you see? I am Christ."

Then Martin, the Spirit revealing the truth to him, that he might understand it was the devil, and not God, replied as follows: "The Lord Jesus did not predict that he would come clothed in purple, and with a glittering crown upon his head. I will not believe that Christ has come, unless he appears with that appearance and form in which he suffered, and openly displaying the marks of his wounds upon the cross."

On hearing these words, the devil vanished like smoke, and filled the cell with such a disgusting smell, that he left unmistakable evidences of his real character. This event, as I have just related, took place in the way which I have stated, and my information regarding it was derived from the lips of Martin himself; therefore let no one regard it as a fable.

CHAPTER XXV

INTERCOURSE OF SULPITIUS WITH MARTIN

For since I, having long heard accounts of his faith, life and virtues, burned with a desire of knowing him, I undertook what was to me a pleasant journey for the purpose of seeing him. At the same time, because already my mind was inflamed with the desire of writing his life, I obtained my information partly from himself, in so far as I could venture to question him, and partly from those who had lived with him, or well knew the facts of the case. And at this time it is scarcely credible with what humility and with what kindness he received me; while he cordially wished me joy, and rejoiced in the Lord that he had been held in such high estimation by me that I had undertaken a journey owing to my desire of seeing him.

Unworthy me! (in fact, I hardly dare acknowledge it), that he should have deigned to admit me to fellowship with him! He went so far as in person to present me with water to wash my hands, and at eventide he himself washed my feet; nor had I sufficient courage to resist or oppose his doing so. In fact, I felt so overcome by the authority he unconsciously exerted, that I deemed it unlawful to do anything but comply with his arrangements. His conversation with me was all directed to such points as the following: that the allurements of this world and secular burdens were to be abandoned in order that we might be free and unencumbered in following the Lord Jesus; and he pressed upon me as an admirable example in present circumstances the conduct of that distinguished man Paulinus, of whom I have made mention above.

Martin declared of him that, by parting with his great possessions and following Christ, as he did, he showed himself almost the only one who in these times had fully obeyed the precepts of the Gospel. He insisted strongly that that was the man who should be made the object of our imitation, adding that the present age was fortunate in possessing such a model of faith and virtue. For Paulinus, being rich and having many possessions, by selling them all and giving them to the poor according to the expressed will of the Lord, had, he said, made possible by actual proof what appeared impossible of accomplishment.

What power and dignity there were in Martin's words and conversation! How active he was, how practical, and how prompt and ready in solving questions connected with Scripture! And because I know that many are incredulous on this point,—for indeed I have met with persons who did not believe me when I related such things,—I call to witness Jesus, and our common hope as Christians, that I never heard from any other lips than those of Martin such exhibitions of knowledge and genius, or such specimens of good and pure speech. But yet, how insignificant is all such praise when compared with the virtues which he possessed! Still, it is remarkable that in a man who had no claim to be called learned, even this attribute [of high intelligence] was not wanting.

CHAPTER XXVI

WORDS CANNOT DESCRIBE THE EXCELLENCES OF MARTIN

But now my book must be brought to an end, and my discourse finished. This is not because all that was worthy of being said concerning Martin is now exhausted, but because I, just as sluggish poets grow less careful towards the end of their work, give over, being baffled by the immensity of the matter. For, although his outward deeds could in some sort of way be set forth in words, no language, I truly own, can ever be capable of describing his inner life and daily conduct, and his mind always bent upon the things of heaven. No one can adequately make known his perseverance and self-mastery in abstinence and fastings, or his power in watchings and prayers, along with the nights, as well as days, which were spent by him, while not a moment was separated from the service of God, either for indulging in ease, or engaging in business. But, in fact, he did not indulge either in food or sleep, except in so far as the necessities of nature required.

I freely confess that, if, as the saying is, Homer himself were to ascend from the shades below, he could not do justice to this subject in words; to such an extent did all excellences surpass in Martin the possibility of being embodied in language. Never did a single hour or moment pass in which he was not either actually engaged in prayer; or, if it happened that he was occupied with something else, still he never let his mind loose from prayer. In truth, just as it is the custom of blacksmiths, in the midst of their work to beat their own anvil as a sort of relief to the laborer, so Martin even when he appeared to be doing something else, was still engaged in prayer.

O truly blessed man in whom there was no guile— judging no man, condemning no man, returning evil for evil to no man! He displayed indeed such marvelous patience in the endurance of injuries, that even when he was chief priest, he allowed himself to be wronged by the lowest clerics with impunity; nor did he either remove them from the office on account of such conduct, or, as far as in him lay, repel them from a place in his affection.

CHAPTER XXVII

WONDERFUL PIETY OF MARTIN

No one ever saw him enraged, or excited, or lamenting, or laughing; he was always one and the same: displaying a kind of heavenly happiness in his countenance, he seemed to have passed the ordinary limits of human nature. Never was there any word on his lips but Christ, and never was there a feeling in his heart except piety, peace, and tender mercy. Frequently, too, he used to weep for the sins of those who showed themselves his revilers—those who, as he led his retired and tranquil life, slandered him with poisoned tongue and a viper's mouth.

And truly we have had experience of some who were envious of his virtues and his life—who really hated in him what they did not see in themselves, and what they had not

power to imitate. And—O wickedness worthy of deepest grief
and groans!—some of his calumniators, although very few,
some of his maligners, I say, were reported to be no others
than bishops! Here, however, it is not necessary to name any
one, although a good many of these people are still venting[4]
their spleen against myself. I shall deem it sufficient that, if
any one of them reads this account, and perceives that he
is himself pointed at, he may have the grace to blush. But
if, on the other hand, he shows anger, he will, by that very
fact, own that he is among those spoken of, though all the
time perhaps I have been thinking of some other person.

I shall, however, by no means feel ashamed if any people
of that sort include myself in their hatred along with such a
man as Martin. I am quite persuaded of this, that the present
little work will give pleasure to all truly good men. And I
shall only say further that, if any one read this narrative in an
unbelieving spirit, he himself will fall into sin. I am conscious
to myself that I have been induced by belief in the facts, and by
the love of Christ, to write these things; and that, in doing so, I
have set forth what is well known, and recorded what is true;
and, as I trust, that man will have a reward prepared by God,
not who shall read these things, but who shall believe them.

---

4   Lit. "are barking round about."

HOW ST. MARTIN PASSED FROM THIS LIFE TO LIFE ETERNAL

Sulpitius Severus sends greetings to Bassula, his venerable parent.

If it were lawful that parents should be summoned to court by their children, clearly I might drag you with a righteous cord before the tribunal of the prætor, on a charge of robbery and plunder. For why should I not complain of the injury which I have suffered at your hands? You have left me no little bit of writing at home, no book, not even a letter—to such a degree do you play the thief with all such things and publish them to the world.

If I write anything in familiar style to a friend; if, as I amuse myself I dictate anything with the wish at the same time that it should be kept private, all such things seem to reach you almost before they have been written or spoken. Surely you have my secretaries in your debt, since through them any trifles I compose are made known to you. And yet I cannot be moved with anger against them if they really obey you, and have invaded my rights under the special influence of your generosity to them, and ever bear in mind that they belong to you rather than to me. Yes, you alone are the culprit—you alone are to blame—inasmuch as you both lay your snares for me, and cajole them with your trickery, so that without making any selection, pieces written familiarly, or let out of hand without care, are sent to you quite unelaborated and unpolished. For, to say nothing about other writings, I beg to ask how that letter could reach you so speedily, which I recently wrote to Aurelius the Deacon.

For, as I was situated at Toulouse, while you were dwelling at Treves, and were so far distant from your native land, owing to the anxiety felt on account of your son, what opportunity, I should like to know, did you avail yourself of, to get hold of that familiar epistle? For I have received your letter in which you write that I ought in the same epistle in which I made mention of the death of our master, Martin, to have described the manner in which that saintly man left this world.

As if, indeed, I had either given forth that epistle with the

view of its being read by any other except him to whom it
purported to be sent; or as if I were fated to undertake so great
a work as that all things which should be known respecting
Martin are to be made public through me particularly as the
writer. Therefore, if you desire to learn anything concerning
the end of the saintly bishop, you should direct your enquiries
rather to those who were present when his death occurred.
I for my part have resolved to write nothing to you lest you
publish me everywhere. Nevertheless if you pledge your word
that you will read to no one what I send you, I shall satisfy
your desire in a few words. Accordingly I shall communicate
to you the following particulars which are comprised within
my own knowledge.

I have to state, then, that Martin was aware of the
period of his own death long before it occurred, and told the
brethren that his departure from the body was at hand. In
the meantime, a reason sprang up which led him to visit the
church at Condate. For, as the clerics of that church were at
variance among themselves, Martin, wishing to restore peace,
although he well knew that the end of his own days was at
hand, yet he did not shrink from undertaking the journey,
with such an object in view.

He did, in fact, think that this would be an excellent

crown to set upon his virtues, if he should leave behind him peace restored to a church. Thus, then, having set out with that very numerous and holy crowd of disciples who usually accompanied him, he perceives in a river a number of water-fowl busy in capturing fishes, and notices that a voracious appetite was urging them on to frequent seizures of their prey. "This," he exclaimed, "is a picture of how the demons act: they lie in wait for the unwary and capture them before they know it: they devour their victims when taken, and they can never be satisfied with what they have devoured." Then Martin, with a miraculous[5] 30 power in his words, commands the birds to leave the pool in which they were swimming, and to betake themselves to dry and desert regions; using with respect to those birds that very same authority with which he had been accustomed to put demons to flight. Accordingly, gathering themselves together, all those birds formed a single body, and leaving the river, they made for the mountains and woods, to no small wonder of many who perceived such power in Martin that he could even rule the birds. Having then delayed some time in that village or church to which he had gone, and peace having been restored among the clerics, when he was now meditating a return to his monastery, he began suddenly to fail in bodily strength, and, assembling the

5   30 "potenti virtute verborum": Halm reads simply "potenti verbo."

brethren, he told them that he was on the point of dissolution. Then indeed, sorrow and grief took possession of all, and there was but one voice of them lamenting, and saying: "Why, dear father, will you leave us? Or to whom can you commit us in our desolation? Fierce wolves will speedily attack your flock, and who, when the shepherd has been smitten, will save us from their bites? We know, indeed, that you desire to be with Christ; but your reward above is safe, and will not be diminished by being delayed; rather have pity upon us, whom you are leaving desolate."

Then Martin, affected by these lamentations, as he was always, in truth, full[6] of compassion, is said to have burst into tears; and, turning to the Lord, he replied to those weeping round him only in the following words, "O Lord, if I am still necessary to Your people, I do not withdraw from toil: Thy will be done." Thus hovering as he did between[7] desire and love, he almost doubted which he preferred; for he neither wished to leave us, nor to be longer separated from Christ.

However, he placed no weight upon his own wishes, nor reserved anything to his own will, but committed himself wholly to the will and power of the Lord. Do you not think

6   32 Lit. "as he always flowed with bowels of mercy in the Lord."

7   33 "spes" seems here to mean "longing of heart."

you hear him speaking in the following few words which I repeat? "Terrible, indeed, Lord, is the struggle of bodily warfare, and surely it is now enough that I have continued the fight till now; but, if You command me still to persevere in the same toil for the defense of Your flock, I do not refuse, nor do I plead against such an appointment my declining years. Wholly given to You, I will fulfill whatever duties You assign me, and I will serve under Your standard as long as You shall prescribe. Surely, although release is sweet to an old man after lengthened toil, yet my mind is a conqueror over my years, and I have no desire to yield to old age. But if now You are merciful to my many years, good, O Lord, is Your will to me; and You Yourself will guard over those for whose safety I fear."

O man, whom no language can describe, unconquered by toil, and unconquerable even by death, who showed no personal preference for either alternative, and who neither feared to die nor refuse to live! Accordingly, though he was for some days under the influence of a strong fever, he nevertheless did not abandon the work of God. Continuing in supplications and watchings through whole nights, he compelled his worn-out limbs to do service to his spirit as he lay on his glorious couch upon sackcloth and ashes. And when his disciples begged of him that at least he should allow some common straw to be placed beneath him, he replied: "It is not fitting that a Christian should die except among ashes; and I have sinned if I leave you a different example."

However, with his hands and eyes steadfastly directed towards heaven, he never released his unconquerable spirit from prayer. And on being asked by the presbyters who had then gathered round him, to relieve his body a little by a change of side, he exclaimed: "Allow me, dear brother, to fix my looks rather on heaven than on earth, so that my spirit which is just about to depart on its own journey may be directed towards the Lord." Having spoken these words, he saw the devil standing close at hand, and exclaimed: "Why do you stand here, you bloody monster? You shall find nothing in me, you deadly one: Abraham's bosom is about to receive me."

As he uttered these words, his spirit fled; and those who were there present have testified to us that they saw his face as if it had been the face of an angel. His limbs too appeared white as snow, so that people exclaimed, "Who would ever believe that man to be clothed in sackcloth, or who would imagine that he was enveloped with ashes?" For even then he presented such an appearance, as if he had been manifested in the glory of the future resurrection, and with the nature of a body that had been changed.

But it is hardly credible what a multitude of human beings assembled at the performance of his funeral rites: the whole city poured forth to meet his body; all the inhabitants of the district and villages, along with many also from the neighboring cities, attended. O how great was the grief of all! How deep the lamentations in particular of the sorrowing monks! They are said to have assembled on that day almost to the number of two thousand,—a special glory of Martin,— through his example so numerous plants had sprung up for the service of the Lord.

Undoubtedly the shepherd was then driving his own flocks before him—the pale crowds of that saintly multitude— bands arrayed in cloaks, either old men whose life-labor was finished, or young soldiers who had just taken the oath of allegiance to Christ. Then, too, there was the choir of virgins, abstaining out of modesty from weeping; and with what holy joy did they conceal the fact of their affliction! No doubt faith would prevent the shedding of tears, yet affection forced out groans.

For there was as sacred an exultation over the glory to which he had attained, as there was a pious sorrow on account of his death. One would have been inclined to pardon those who wept, as well as to congratulate those who rejoiced, while each single person preferred that he himself should grieve, but that another should rejoice. Thus then this multitude, singing hymns of heaven, attended the body of the sainted man onwards to the place of the tomb. Let there be compared with this spectacle, I will not say the worldly pomp of a funeral, but even of a triumph; and what can be reckoned similar to the obsequies of Martin? Let your worldly great men lead before their chariots captives with their hands bound behind their backs. Those accompanied the body of Martin who, under his guidance, had overcome the world. Let madness honor these earthly warriors with the united praises of nations. Martin is praised with the divine psalms, Martin is honored in heavenly hymns.

Those worldly men, after their triumphs here are over, shall be thrust into cruel Tartarus, while Martin is joyfully received into the bosom of Abraham. Martin, poor and insignificant on earth, has a rich entrance granted him into heaven. From that blessed region, as I trust, he looks upon me, as my guardian, while I am writing these things, and upon you while you read them.

CPSIA information can be obtained
at www.ICGtesting.com
Printed in the USA
BVOW08s1116291217
503975BV00001B/67/P

9 780987 340047